Leabharlann Dhún Chathair Chorcaí

3 0007 00198 941 6

KU-366-159

Cork City Libraries
WITHDRAWN
FROM STOCK

172172

Poems about
Food

Selected by
Amanda Earl & Danielle Sensier

**Illustrated by
Frances Lloyd**

Wayland

Titles in the series
Poems about . . .

Animals	**Food**
Colours	**Growth**
Day & Night	**Homes**
Families	**Journeys**
Feelings	**Weather**

ST. MARY'S ROAD BRANCH

For Colette and Isabel

Series editor: Catherine Baxter
Designer: Loraine Hayes

First published in 1994 by
Wayland (Publishers) Ltd
61 Western Road, Hove
East Sussex BN3 1JD, England

Typeset by Dorchester Typesetting
Group Ltd, Dorset, England.
Printed and bound in Italy by
G. Canale & C.S.p.A, Turin.

© Copyright 1994 Wayland
(Publishers) Ltd

British Library Cataloguing in Publication Data

Poems About Food. – (Poems About . . .
Series)
  I. Earl, Amanda II. Sensier, Danielle
III. Series
808.819355

ISBN 0-7502-1037-0

170160 CORK CITY LIBRARY

Front cover: Boy eating chips/design: S. Balley

Poets' nationalities

Grace Nichols	Guyanese
Michael Rosen	English
Else Holmelund Minarik	German/American
Patricia Hubbell	American
Ogden Nash	American
Zhenya Gay	American
Roger McGough	English
John Agard	British/Guyanese
Stanley Cook	English
Quentin Blake	English
Kit Wright	English
Christina Rossetti	English/Italian
Leland B. Jacobs	American

Contents

I'm a Banana Man

I'm a banana man
I just love shaking
those yellow hands
yes man

Banana in the morning
Banana in the evening
Banana before I go to bed
at night, that's right
that's how much I love
the Banana Bite

I'm a banana man
not a Superman
or a Batman
or a Spiderman
no man

Banana in the morning
Banana in the evening
Banana before I go to bed
at night, that's right
that's how much I love
the Banana Bite

Grace Nichols

Bee

You want to make some honey?
All right. Here's the recipe.
Pour the juice of a thousand flowers
Through the sweet tooth of a bee.

X. J. Kennedy

6

My Brother

my brother's on the floor roaring
my brother's on the floor roaring
why is my brother on the floor roaring?
my brother is on the floor roaring
because he's supposed to finish his beans
before he has his pudding

but he doesn't want to finish his beans
before he has his pudding

he says he wants his pudding
NOW

but they won't let him

so now my brother is on the floor roaring

they're saying
I give you one more chance to finish those beans
or you don't go to Tony's
but he's not listening
because he's on the floor roaring

he's getting told off
I'm not
I've eaten my beans
and do you know what I'm doing now?
I'm eating my pudding
and he's on the floor roaring

if he wasn't on the floor roaring
he'd see me eating my pudding
if he looked really close
he might see a little tiny smile
just at the corner of my mouth
but he's not looking.
he's on the floor roaring.

the pudding is OK
it's not wonderful
not wonderful enough
to be sitting on the floor and roaring about –
unless you're my brother

Michael Rosen

Little Seeds

Little seeds we sow in spring,
growing while the robins sing,
give us carrots, peas and beans,
tomatoes, pumpkins, squash* and greens.

And we pick them,
one and all,
through the summer,
through the fall.

Winter comes, then spring, and then
little seeds we sow again.

Else Holmelund Minarik

* a vegetable

Lemons

A lemon's a lemony kind of thing,
It doesn't look sharp and it doesn't look sting,
It looks rather round and it looks rather square,
It looks almost oval, a yellowy pear.

It looks like a waxy old, yellow old pear,
It looks like a pear without any stem,
It doesn't look sharp and it doesn't look sting,
A lemon's a lemony kind of thing.

But cut it and taste it and touch it with tongue
You'll see where the sharp and the sting have been hiding –
Under the yellow without any warning;
I touch it and touch it again with my tongue,
I like it! I like it! I like to be stung.

Patricia Hubbell

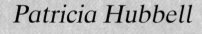

A Peanut

A peanut sat on the railroad track,
His heart was all a-flutter.
Along came a train, the 10.15 –
Toot-toot! peanut butter!

Anonymous

Mustard

I'm mad about mustard –
Even on custard.

Ogden Nash

Peas

I always eat peas with honey,
I've done it all my life,
They do taste kind of funny
But it keeps them on the knife.

Anonymous

The silver rain

The Silver Rain
The Shining Sun
The fields where scarlet poppies run

And all the ripples of the wheat
Are in the bread that I do eat
And when I sit for every meal
And say a grace I always feel
That I am eating rain and sun in
The fields where scarlet poppies run.

Yasmin Isaacs
(aged 10)

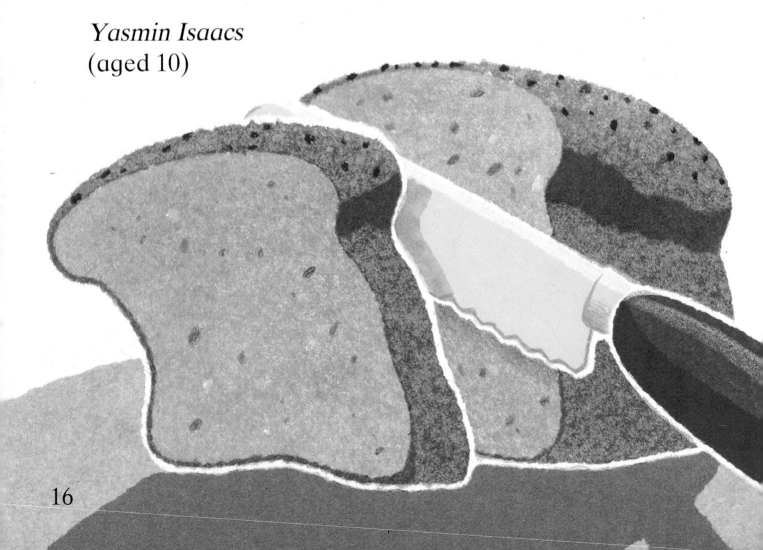

Tuna Sandwiches

I want you
I want you
I want you
na sandwiches

I want you
I want you
I want you
na sandwiches

chew chew chew
na sandwiches

chew chew chew
na sandwiches

Roger Mc Gough

In the Summer We Eat

In the summer we eat,
in the winter we don't;
In the summer we'll play,
in the winter we won't.
All the winter we sleep, each curled in a ball
As soon as the snowflakes start to fall.
But in the spring we each come out of our den
And start to eat all over again.

Zhenya Gay

**The Hardest thing to do
in the World**
is standing in the hot sun
at the end of a long queue for ice creams
watching all the people who've just bought theirs
coming away from the queue
giving their ice creams their very first lick.

Michael Rosen

Snow-cone

Snow-cone nice
Snow-cone sweet
Snow-cone is crush ice
and good for the heat.

When sun really hot
and I thirsty a lot,
Me alone,
Yes me alone,
could eat ten snow-cone.
If you think is lie I tell

wait till you hear the snow-cone bell,
wait till you hear the snow-cone bell.

John Agard

21

Chips

Out of the paper bag
Comes the hot breath of the chips
And I shall blow on them
To stop them burning my lips.

Before I leave the counter
The woman shakes
Raindrops of vinegar on them
And salty snowflakes.

Outside the frosty pavements
Are slippery as a slide
But the chips and I
Are warm inside.

Stanley Cook

Sorting Out the Kitchen Pans

We're sorting out the Kitchen Pans
    DING DONG BANG
Sorting out the Kitchen Pans
    BING BONG CLANG

Sorting out the Kitchen Pans
    TING BANG DONG
Sorting out the Kitchen Pans
    CLANG DING BONG

Sorting out the Kitchen Pans
    DONG DANG BONG
TING TANG BING BANG
    CLANG DING
           OW!

Quentin Blake

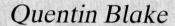

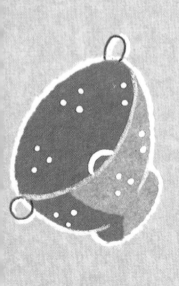

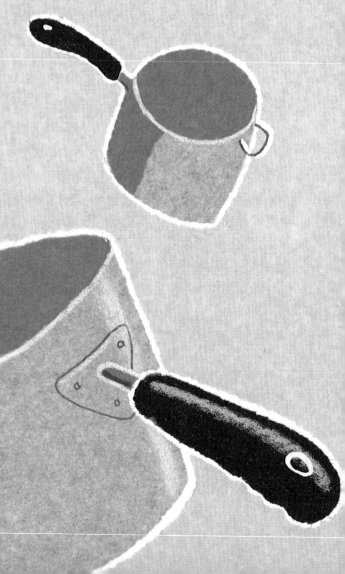

If you're no good at cooking

If you're no good at cooking,
Can't fry or bake,

Here's something you
Can always make. Take

Three very ordinary
slices of bread:

Stack the second
On the first one's head.

Stack the third
On top of that.

There! Your three slices
Lying pat.
So what have you got?
A BREAD SANDWICH,

That's what!
Why not?

Kit Wright

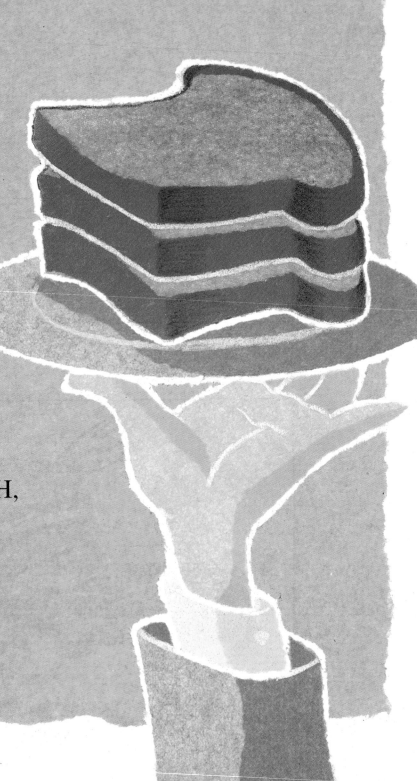

Mix a Pancake

Mix a pancake,
Stir a pancake,
Pop it in the pan;
Fry a pancake,
Toss the pancake –
Catch it if you can.

Christina Rossetti

Taste of Purple

Grapes hang purple
In their bunches,
Ready for
September lunches.
Gather them, no
Minutes wasting.
Purple is
Delicious tasting.

Leland B. Jacobs

CORK CITY LIBRARY

How to use this book

Poetry is a very enjoyable area of literature and children
take to it naturally, usually beginning with nursery rhymes.
It's what happens next that can make all the difference!
This series of thematic poetry anthologies keeps poetry
alive and enjoyable for young children.

When using these books there are several ways in which
you can help a child to appreciate poetry and to understand the
ways in which words can be carefully chosen and sculpted
to convey different atmospheres and meanings. Try to
encourage the following:

- Joining in when the poem is read out loud.
- Talking about favourite words, phrases or images.
- Discussing the illustration and photographs.
- Miming facial expressions to suit the mood of the poems.
- Acting out events in the poems.
- Copying out the words.
- Learning favourite poems by heart.
- Discussing the difference between a poem and a story
- Clapping hands to rhythmic poems
- Talking about metaphors/similes eg what kind of weather
  would a lion be? What colour would sadness be? What
  would it taste like? If you could hold it, how would it
  feel?

It is inevitable that, at some point, children will want to
write poems themselves. Writing a poem is, however, only
one way of enjoying poetry. With the above activities,
children can be encouraged to appreciate and delight in
this unique form of communication.

Picture acknowledgements

APM Studios cover, 23; Cephas 20 (John Heinrich), 28 (Ted Stefanski); Life File 4 (Richard Powers), 7 (Paul Richards), 11 (John Cox), 18 (Mike Potter), 25 (Emma Lee); Science Photo Library 12 (John Mead); Zefa 17.

Text acknowledgements

For permission to reprint copyright material the publishers gratefully acknowledge the following: John Agard c/o Caroline Sheldon Literary Agency for 'Snow-Cone' from *Another Very First Poetry Book* by John Agard, published by Oxford University Press. Reprinted by permission of the author; Curtis Brown Group Ltd UK for 'I'm a Banana Man' from *Come On Into My Tropical Garden* by Grace Nicholls. Copyright © Grace Nicholls 1988. Reprinted by permission of Curtis Brown Group Ltd; Curtis Brown US Ltd for 'Bee' from *Did Adam Name the Vinagaroon* by X. J. Kennedy. Copyright © 1982 X. J. Kennedy, published by David Godine Publishers. 'Mustard' from *Everyone But Thee, Me and Thee* by Ogden Nash, published by Little Brown & Co Copyright © 1962 Ogden Nash. Reprinted by permission of Curtis Brown US Ltd; Henry Holt & Co Inc for 'A Taste of Purple' from *Is Somewhere Always Far Away* by Leland B. Jacobs. Copyright © 1967 Leland B. Jacobs. Reprinted by permission of Henry Holt & Co Inc; Sarah Matthews for 'Chips' by Stanley Cook; The National Exhibition of Children's Art for 'The Silver Rain' by Yasmin Issacs; Penguin Books Ltd for 'The Hardest thing to do in the World' from *You Tell Me* by Michael Rosen. Copyright © Michael Rosen 1979. First published by Viking Children's Books. Peters, Fraser & Dunlop for 'My Brother' from *A World of Poetry* by Michael Rosen. Reprinted by permission of Peters Fraser & Dunlop Group Ltd; Peters Fraser & Dunlop Group Ltd for 'Tuna Sandwiches' from *Pillow Talk* by Roger McGough. Published by Penguin Books Ltd; Random House UK Ltd for 'Sorting Out the Kitchen Pans' by Quentin Blake from *All Join In*, published by Jonathan Cape.

While every effort has been made to secure permission, in some cases it has proved impossible to trace the copyright holders. The publishers apologise for this apparent negligence.

Index of first lines